KC MCCORMICK ÇIFTÇI

The K-1 Visa Wedding Plan

An interactive guide to marrying your international fiance(e) in 90 days

BORDERLESS
S T O R I E S

Contents

Client Testimonials

KC was so full of patience and sound advice. She helped me to differentiate the major life stressors that I can control versus those that I do not have control over. This process allowed me to regain a sense of control throughout what has been an incredibly hectic and uncertain time in both mine and my fiance's lives. I feel like KC also helped me to understand the genuine importance of making sure to take care of myself and relationship during this difficult season. She provided so much practical, step by step advice that was easy to follow through on. You have been an enormous support—it's such a gift knowing that someone else understands!

-Carrie & Juan

Finding Borderless Stories and working with KC while going through the K-1 process was everything I had been searching the internet for and could never seem to find. I discovered the K-1 Visa Wedding Plan just before I filed for my now husband and it gave me some really good things to start thinking through and the fact that it was coming from someone who had been through this all already was priceless. Shortly after finding that course I joined the membership community which was another added layer of support. It was amazing to have what felt like a friend and a mentor who knew first hand what this process was like as well as an awesome group of ladies some of which were going through the K-1 process at the same time. It gave me a community of people who understood me in a way that so many other people could not!

–Holly

1

Introduction

Welcome to the K-1 Visa Wedding Plan e-book. I'm your instructor, friend, and guide, KC McCormick Çiftçi. I went through the K-1 visa process with my husband in 2016 and we've been living in the US ever since we got him his visa, got married and did all of those fun things that I'm sure you're in the midst of right now.

In case you don't already know, the K-1 visa is a visa that's issued to the non-citizen fiance(e) of a US citizen, and it allows that person to enter the US and marry his or her citizen fiance(e) within 90 days.

So, what's the problem facing couples in this process? Why did I feel the need to write this e-book in the first place?

Well, the K-1 visa process is a long stressful time in a relationship and when you add wedding planning into that as well, it can really shoot that stress level through the roof. I don't want that for you. The goal of this e-book is to help you navigate that time of waiting and wedding planning with as much celebration of your relationship as possible and as little stress and worry.

Who is this book for?

It's for anyone who's in the K-1 process or thinking about beginning the K-1 process. So without further ado, let's jump right in.

2

Preparing Your Application

To start from the true beginning, we're talking about preparing your application. Nothing else happens if you don't first prepare your application. Let's get right into it.

Do you need an immigration lawyer?

The first question you need to answer is whether or not you need an immigration lawyer or not. Many people are able to go through the K-1 application process on their own, but at times it is recommended to have an immigration lawyer. Some of the questions that are worth answering include:

Are you or your partner from a country considered "high fraud" by USCIS?

This ("high fraud") is the language used by USCIS and on the visa forums. I don't say this to be derogatory about any countries, just to use the designated terminology. This description is applied to countries where USCIS tends to have more cases of fraud in applications for fiance visas and spousal visas. So, in these countries it can be more difficult to get that visa. It is important to know this and to be realistic about it. And in the case where it is a high fraud country, it doesn't necessarily mean you do need a lawyer, but you do need to be more careful about following all the steps in the application process because there will be additional requirements.

What is your personal history (past visas, criminal history, etc.)?

This is a plural "you" here, referring to both you and your partner in terms of past visas, criminal history, et cetera. What I mean by this is if the US citizen in this case has been married in the past and those marriages were fiance visa marriages as well, then your case will be looked at with more scrutiny than if this is the first marriage for both of you. Additionally, if there are other visas at play here, like maybe if the partner who is not a citizen has overstayed a tourist visa or has misused any kind of visa that they were granted to the US in the past, they might also have potential issues with their application. In those cases it might be helpful to have an immigration lawyer. Criminal history should also be considered as well as those are things that are asked on the application about any records of serious crimes. If you have indiscretions in your past, either one of you, that could potentially prevent you from from being together, then it might be worth seeking legal help.

What is your comfort level with the language used in the application?

The application is written in legalese, so there are things that take a lot of decoding even for someone who speaks English as a first language. If English is not your first language or if you are just not comfortable with decoding the messages there, it might be helpful to hire someone, either a lawyer to help you or to go through a service that will process your application for you if it will give you peace of mind.

Are you prepared for the expense of hiring an immigration lawyer?

This is not a cheap thing to do, so you'll need to consider your budget for the visa process. It is expensive. We'll touch on the exact expenses later as a little bit of a reality check, but if you're considering hiring a lawyer, then you need to figure that into your budget as well and see if you can absorb the expense. If you're going to end up not being able to pay your rent but it would just take a little more work for you to do the application yourself, then I wouldn't say it's necessarily required. You certainly don't have to have a lawyer, despite what people might tell you. This is something I experienced — when they learned my fiance wasn't from the US, many people assumed that I had a lawyer or told me I had to get a lawyer and that just wasn't the case for us.

Hiring a lawyer

I would not say that everyone needs to have a lawyer to go through this process, so don't take it as a given from fresh out of the gate. I can't legally advise you either way, so this is a question for you and your partner to work through together. This is a personal decision and it depends on a lot of different circumstances as far as hiring a lawyer.

Ask for local recommendations on immigration forums

I'm not going to make any specific recommendations here because the reality is that you're likely going to want a local recommendation. You might not want to work with somebody on the Internet, though that's certainly an option. But you might want to be able to connect with them in real life, and if you need any legal support with your interviews or with gathering anything that can be done face to face, then you might want it to be somebody who's local. In that case, I'd recommend asking on the immigration forums for somebody in your city or general area. I don't know anyone myself that I could recommend and I don't think it would be very ethical for me to advise you to work with someone just because I have a deal or a relationship with them.

Consider visa processing services if they will meet your needs

You can also consider sites like RapidVisa or Boundless. Those are two examples that I've seen in my time on the Internet, which are not legal help but they are visa processing services. If that will meet your needs and if that's worthwhile for you to do, it is another expense, but it could be something that might give you peace of mind. So look into it, maybe ask around on forums to see if people have used those services and if they found them helpful. I do know that they're both partners on VisaJourney, which is my favorite forum that I'll be telling you about soon. Maybe that means VisaJourney is vouching for them, though I wouldn't necessarily assume that. I would ask for experiences, testimonials and see if it is necessary for you.

Doing it yourself

Of course you can also do it yourself. I tend to be a fan of DIYing things, but I would never ever say in the case of immigration and legal matters that everyone must do it this way. Nope, that's not the case, but if you decide to, this is my advice for how to do that.

Use visa forums

First and foremost you need to be on visa forums. My favorite one, as you probably know if you've heard me talk at all about this process is called VisaJourney.com and it's incredibly helpful. Why? Well, I'm glad you asked. So there is information that is tailored to the embassy where your application is being processed. Yes, in addition to all of the information that you need for your I-129F application that's required by the US government, there are also additional requirements and things to be aware of depending on the embassy where your application is being processed and where you are going to be having your interview. This can vary wildly from country to country, especially in countries considered high fraud, where the requirements can be a lot more stringent. In countries that are not considered high fraud, they might be more lax, but you can't know for sure unless you get on a forum and talk to somebody who is in the same position that you are. You can also find some information on the embassy website, so I would advise to do both of those things. **Look at the embassy website and their K-1 requirements and also ask on the forums for the most recent experiences that people have had.** These things can be really helpful.

Compare timelines

Another thing that is great about forums and very helpful is that you see others' timelines for their visa journey. I know when I was using the visa forums, I updated it in terms of the date that we send our application, the date we received our first notice of action, second notice of action and so on and so forth, and I could see other people who applied at the same time as me and where they were at in terms of getting that second notice of action. Because of their information, I had more of an idea of when ours was coming. I realize it is possible to find a timeline estimate on the USCIS website as well, though it does tend to be more conservative. Of course they don't want to give people reason to worry that their application isn't being processed fast enough, so the estimates will give you more of a worst case scenario for when you should start worrying that you haven't heard anything and when it would be acceptable for you to pick up the phone and call them. There's no need for them to needlessly alarm people like that.

So it's helpful to see others' experiences and they can also share reviews of their interview at the specific embassy. They'll tell you about what that was like and you can help prepare yourself. Maybe you know that, for example, you can't bring a bag inside the embassy, which was the case for my husband. He ended up having to leave his backpack at a convenience store across across the way, which was fine. Apparently that's what everybody was doing, but it would have been nice if he could have known that and that kind of information would generally be in those reviews. It was just a recent change for him and that's why he didn't know about it. It worked out fine, but we all like to prepare for things and a great way to prepare is to hear someone else's story.

Kindness of strangers

Additionally, I've found that the willingness of others to help on those forums is really incredible. I know I asked questions on there when we were at various stages in our process. When I was sending financial documents to my fiance in Turkey and they got lost in the mail twice, that's the first place I turned to say, "Oh my gosh, what, what do I do? What else can I do?" Everyone was very helpful and offered alternative solutions and it ended up working out fine. Even initially introducing myself on there and sharing where we were in the process and asking about the path ahead was very helpful. I was able to connect with other people who had fiances in Turkey and it was just really wonderful to see that. I never felt like anybody was frustrated or impatient with my "stupid" questions. They were always helpful in at least pointing me in the right direction if the question had already been answered somewhere else.

Peace of mind

It was also just great for peace of mind. There's a lot of silence in the waiting in the K-1 process. When you receive your first notice of action, that's great. You know they've gotten your documents, things are moving, but then it can be a few months before you get a second notice of action and you don't hear anything in the meantime. So it can really help to connect with others in the same position and know that you're on the same page and things are moving forward even if you can't see it for yourself.

Remember to share responsibility

One piece of advice that I have for the K-1 process, especially if you decide to do it yourself, is to remember to share responsibility for the process as a whole. Even if one of you takes more on, in terms of collecting all the documents, filling out all the paperwork, researching all the things that you need to know, like your addresses for the past years and all of that kind of stuff, it is really important to share their responsibility. **Let it be something that brings you together. Let it be something that bonds you as a couple.** The alternative to that is that if one of you takes on responsibility, it becomes way too easy for that to be a source of conflict and blaming each other if something goes wrong.

Let's imagine that one of you fills out the paperwork all on his or her own, and let's call that person Susie. If Susie fills out all that paperwork all by herself and gets no help from her partner, she might feel fine and think, "Okay, I filled it all out. Everything's great. It's all going to work," but then if there is a problem, then Susie might blame herself. She might blame her partner for not helping her and her partner might blame her for not doing a good enough job. And then she might blame him back, saying, "Well, why didn't you help me more?" It can become something pretty ugly if that happens and there's no need to start off your marriage that way or potentially end your relationship that way.

This can be as simple as making a checklist, going through it once yourself and making sure all the documents are there, and then going through that checklist with your partner. You can take that checklist and those documents to your partner and say, "All right, I have *this* to meet this requirement, I have *this* to meet that requirement," and so on. It makes you feel more confident by explaining it out loud — they do say the best way to learn something is to explain it to someone else. But it also helps your partner be a fresh set of eyes looking at it and saying, "Oh, that doesn't make sense," or, "You missed a signature there." That's something that can easily happen. With pages and pages of documents, it can be easy to miss a signature and that is not something that you want to have delay you being able to be together.

Evidence to start saving

My recommendation is to make a big old list of the evidence that you need to gather with your application. Now this is going to be in its most up to date form if you go to the USCIS website and look at the K-1 application and the instructions that come with it. Later you will also need to look at the embassy specific requirements, which you will find on the embassy website and also you can have conversation about that on the visa forums. I'd say it doesn't hurt to look at the embassy-specific information now, as well, so that you can have one master list of all the paperwork that you need.

Primary evidence

As far as assembling your application, one thing to be aware of is to focus your efforts first and foremost on having primary evidence. This is going to be official documents like stamps in your passport that show that you entered your partner's country (or vice versa) on this date and left on this date. That's what they want to see to know that you at least were in the same country, which becomes evidence that you did meet in person.

As you're probably aware, there is a requirement that you've met in person within two years prior to your application, so passport stamps go a long way to show that. Additionally, flight tickets fall into this category. If the two of you ever travel someplace together, keep those tickets that show that you're both traveled on an airplane sitting next to each other. It's a great way to show that you're in the same place at the same time. If you have been able to live together, your lease or any kind of official document like that certainly counts as evidence. Of course if you have children, those birth certificates are essential. Naturally you don't need to, you know, go have a child just to prove that you're in a relationship. I certainly don't recommend that, but I'm just saying if you do have anything official, I highly, highly recommend focusing your attention on that first.

Secondary evidence is secondary

Secondary evidence is something that we tend to get more distracted by and think we need a ton of, but it is secondary for a reason. This includes photos of the two of you together, notes or chat logs of your communications or letters and affidavits from people who know you and who can vouch for you. This is not as important as the official stuff. You should still include an appropriate amount of it, but don't weigh your application too heavily with it because the reality is that these are things that that can be recreated. If the Internet has taught us anything, it's that we shouldn't trust a lot of what we see, and the people processing your application know this just as well as you do. **It should go without saying, but absolutely do not fabricate any parts of your application.** Be aware that the secondary evidence that you do have isn't weighted as heavily by the people conducting interviews and processing applications because it's secondary. My advice here is don't overdo it with secondary evidence. Include it, absolutely. But be clear on what is required and stick with those guidelines. If you decide, for example that you want to include every photo ever taken of the two of you (and you've spent a lot of time together, it's not like you just met once or twice) and you include with your application a whole bound document that is 200 pages of photos of you, think about the person receiving that document. Potentially that person might think it's cute — but they might also be frustrated by it. And I think the last thing you want to do is to frustrate the person who's processing your application. In closing this chapter, let me just say that there's no need to draw attention to yourself because you failed to follow instructions. Read those instructions and follow them to the letter of the law.

Exercises

Do you need to hire an immigration lawyer, or can you do it yourself?

1. What documents and evidence do you need to include with the I-129F? Check the USCIS website for up-to-date instructions.

2. What documents and evidence do you need to prepare specific to your embassy? Check the embassy website and visa forums for up-to-date information.

3. What secondary evidence will help support the primary evidence listed above? Check USCIS and the visa forums, but be sure your primary evidence is intact and you aren't relying too heavily on secondary

evidence.

3

The Waiting Game

The next stage is the waiting game. This is the part when you are separated and this most likely happens in some form for all of us. Many couples are already in a long distance relationship leading up to this and many others like myself and my husband were together in his country, but then were separated when I returned to the US to figure out our living and job situation. So this is what we call the waiting game, also known as long distance relationship time. Fun, fun.

Long distance love

How does long distance love work, anyway? How do you manage to nurture a long distance relationship? I'm sure some of you who are reading this have been long distance for quite a long time and you might say, "KC, what could you possibly have to teach me at this point?" And that's certainly a valid point. I'm sure many of you are experts and I have nothing but admiration for the months or years some of you have spent in a long distance relationship. I know for me it was a short time as my husband and I happened to be together in Turkey in the very beginning of our relationship and were only separated for a few months during the visa process when I was looking for a job. That said, there are still things that I learned during that time and have learned from talking with others who are in long distance relationships that may be helpful to you.

One of the most important things, and I've said it before and I will definitely say it again, is to be sure that you're nurturing your relationship during this time. Maybe before you started the K-1 process, you had more fun together and now that you're in this stressful visa process, you have a lot of conversations about the stressful visa process.

Here's how I like to think about it. If you're familiar with Pavlov and classical conditioning, you might already know this, but I'm going to summarize it briefly here just in case. Pavlov conditioned a dog by ringing a bell every time he fed it. At some point the dog began to salivate just when he heard the bell ringing. Right now you may be thinking, "KC, what does this have to do with my international fiance?" My point is if every time you see your partner, you're talking about something stressful, it could potentially become a situation similar to that of Pavlov's dog where every time your name pops up on the phone screen your partner immediately feels anxious and wonders, "What did I do wrong? What's the problem now? What's going to happen?"

I'm not saying you should never talk about the visa process, of course. Obviously you need to make sure you get through it, so you need to talk about it, but make sure that you intentionally have fun and you have conversations that aren't all stress all the time. Remember to have fun and enjoy hanging out, even if it's long distance.

Communication

The most important skill in a long distance relationship is definitely communication. One piece of advice about communication specific to the K-1 process is to have one main platform for texting. That way you can create a chat log to show evidence of an ongoing relationship when the non-citizen partner goes to the interview. Be sure that you're texting on a platform that's going to save your chat long and allow you to download it and print it out for secondary evidence. I think when we were using WhatsApp it was tricky to figure out how to do that and we needed to use the desktop version but didn't have access to it. So there ended up being pages and pages of screenshots, which isn't ideal, though it did work. There's no need to be alarmed if you've already got months of chats saved as screenshots — it works. But if you're just starting out and if it's possible to do something that can be downloaded and have timestamps and profile pictures, that would be really helpful.

Of course, don't just get so focused on having the conversations to show that you're having an ongoing relationship that you forget to change it up and do something fun, spontaneous, and interesting. It's important to find ways to communicate and show love that are different than the norm. Maybe you kind of get in a rut. You may find yourself in the same routine day in, day out, and nobody really wants their relationship to be routine, right? You don't want it to feel like it's just another responsibility that you have to check off of your to-do list: make your bed, brush your teeth, and be sure to text your fiance. Yes, it's important to be committed to each other, and to talk as often as you possibly can, but why not change things up a little bit from time to time? So, maybe drop a postcard in the mail or a little gift or send a letter. Do whatever comes to your mind. I'm pretty sure even if your partner's love language isn't words, we all like getting mail, right? Maybe you don't like sending snail mail or are afraid it'll get lost in the mail. Well, then make a cute little e-card in Paint or something and send it to your partner. Who doesn't like that? (Probably a graphic designer.) But honestly, even if they're a graphic designer, if they love you, they'll still think a card made in Paint is cute.

It's also important to do things just because. After all, you're building a relationship that's ideally going to last you for the rest of your life.

You don't want to sacrifice the foundational building blocks that are going to carry you through the decades to come. Make sure that you are having fun and you're surprising each other in good ways. Sometimes bad surprises happen, like a request for additional evidence or a delay in being reunited. So why not throw a good surprise into the mix? You could have a pizza delivered to your partner's house. That might be a bad example — maybe your partner isn't home because they're at work and you had a pizza delivered and it's cold now, but hey, you know them better than I do. You know what they might like. You can get creative and there are so, so, so, so many ways to do that. Sometimes you enlist the help of their friends and family who are local to surprise them in a sweet and creative way. Think about some fun things that you could do, jot down some ideas, and see if you can surprise yourself, even.

Day to day

I also recommend trying to include each other in your day to day as much as possible. It's really nice in a time of separation, especially for those of you who might just be separated now. Maybe, like me and my husband, you were together in your partner's country but now you're back in the US waiting for them to join you and you're separated for the first time. Then as your life is changing, and as your partner's life is changing without you there, it's important to talk about what's happening day to day. Do you have a new job? Do you have new coworkers? Are you seeing your family more? These are things that are going to matter when you're together again and you say, "I'm going to work with so and so" and they don't know who you're talking about. What do you say? "Oh yeah, I guess I didn't mention this whole part of my life to you because we were just focusing on other stuff." So as much as you can take an interest in your partner's day, also share your time with him or her.

Of course, it's also important to remember (and this is a life lesson), that at the end of a long day, you always want to check in and make sure you're ready to listen to each other. Maybe you've both had a long day, so you can ask, "Are you ready for me to vent right now? Are you ready for me to share this with you?" Because it can be even harder when you're long distance and you're limited to texting or FaceTiming and you're just feeling tired and exhausted and maybe even a little bit cranky. Especially then, it's important to check in and to make sure that someone else is ready to take on your emotions and your feelings and hear about all of this stuff that you're going through. And of course then we need to return the favor and offer a listening ear or comforting shoulder.

Nurture your relationship

Finally, do not forget to nurture your relationship. Be sure that you talk about things other than the K-1 process. Talk about your day, talk about life, talk about your beliefs, talk about philosophy, or even talk about politics. You know, normally they say not to talk about politics or religion, but if you're going to marry somebody, I think you're going to talk about those things at some point. Talk about your future together. Talk about a movie you watched. There are a lot of things to talk about and the K-1 process should just be one of them.

Share responsibility

How many times can I say this? Please remember to share responsibility during this time. Neither one of you is in this alone. You're in it together, and it is kind of a big test of your relationship. Couples who are from the same country don't really have the same hoops to jump through to be together, so I like to think going through this process makes us stronger. So let it be that, **let it be something that brings you together and not**

something that becomes a major source of conflict for years to come.

Do your homework

I'll also remind you to do your homework, and don't worry, it's fun homework. In this context, doing your homework means collecting additional things to put in that "evidence of an ongoing relationship" file. This can mean whatever you want it to mean. You can hang out on a video chat and watch YouTube videos together and screenshot it. That can be one little piece of secondary evidence. If you are able to take a trip to see each other, then by all means, do that. That's really powerful primary evidence right there. The evidence of an ongoing relationship just comes from having an ongoing relationship, so do what is natural that you've already been doing. Continue to communicate and spend time together in whatever ways you're able to do and just make sure that you're collecting it and putting it in a file folder. That's going to be really helpful when it comes time for that interview.

Take care of yourself

Don't forget to look out for yourself in this time of stress and anxiety. This is a challenging time. I know that from my experience and I know that from the the women that I've had the privilege of working with. There are many unknowns up in the air, including whether the visa will be granted or not, maybe things like where you will live or where you will work, what options the non-citizen partner will have a for work in the US, maybe some pressure from family on both sides, and maybe even a strained relationship from being long distance. It's a lot to work through, and it's a lot to think about. So, the most important thing that you can do for you is to take care of you, whatever that means.

Self care is not just taking a bubble bath and putting on a face mask.

Sure, those are a great way to communicate to your body and to yourself, "I care about you, I value you. I want you to keep on ticking, keep on moving forward." But it's also important to eat healthy food, get enough sleep, and process your emotions. Maybe that means writing down the things that you're feeling. Even if you say, "I'm not somebody who likes to write," well you know what? Anybody can journal. There's no right or wrong way to do it, but getting all those thoughts and feelings out of your head onto a piece of paper where you can release it is really powerful. It can help you to set free the ideas that are causing you stress and sometimes worries that seem monumental are actually tiny when you see them down on paper.

As another component of self care, find somebody to talk to about this process other than your partner. When there's stress and pain, it's good to get a fresh perspective and to not make your partner feel like he or she is the cause of that stress and pain. So while you have fun with them, you can also have a friend or a parent or a sibling or cousin or a friendly coworker or a mental health professional that you can share with who can understand them. Of course, our Borderless Stories community is a great place for that too, as many of us are in the same situation and are able to relate to what's going on so you don't have to explain yourself quite as much as you might with a family member.

Exercises

How can you get creative with your communication while you're apart?

Write down some ideas about how you can date and have fun while you're far apart, nurturing your relationship during this (extra) stressful time.

4

Master Your Mindset

This chapter has some of the ideas I'm most excited to share with you. When we really get into understanding our own beliefs and thoughts, we can learn how they influence the way we move through this world, and that's certainly true during the K-1 process and intercultural relationships in general.

Visualize your perfect wedding day...

We're going to start with an exercise here around shifting your mindset around your wedding. Feel free to read what I've written here and then close your eyes and try to picture it and then jot some of those ideas down in your journal.

I want you to visualize that wedding day that you've always dreamed about. Now right there, you might be reacting by saying either, "Excuse me, KC, I have never dreamed of a wedding in my whole life," or you might think, "Oh my gosh yes, I've been prepared for this since I had my first crush ever, I have so many things to write down!" Wherever on that spectrum you fall, you probably have at least a few thoughts and some feelings about what a wedding looks like. You've probably been to weddings, and you've surely seen movies where people were getting married. Think of those things. Think of what it is deep inside you that you think is a perfect wedding. What would you wear? What would your partner wear? Who is there? What kind of food are you eating? What does your cake look like? What kind of gifts are people giving you? All of those things. Anything that you like, and especially the things that you can't even imagine having an alternative option. Think about it, write it down, say it out loud to your empty room right now. Hold it in your mind. Picture it. Visualize it.

Did you do it? Awesome!

Now, scrap it. If you wrote it on a scrap of paper, you can crumple it up. No need to light it on fire or anything like that (and especially not if you wrote it right here in the book!), but you can do something symbolic to show that you're stepping away from it. Maybe draw an "X" over the page. The important thing is communicating to yourself that you are releasing it and letting it go.

Now bear with me, if this is making you feel uncomfortable or angry. All I want you to do right now is to realize or remember that **there's**

nothing more important about your wedding than the actual change that's happening, which is the beginning of a marriage.

The reality in a situation like ours where you are separated by probably one ocean or maybe even two is that the chances of getting all of these perfect details together in time for one single day are very small. The thought that in this short span of time, I'm going to have that designer gown and I'm going to have a cake from some famous, fancy cake place, and I'm going to get all of my friends together to be a massive wedding party where everyone is wearing coordinated outfits and... and....and....it's all going to be perfect and beautiful and wonderful.

It can happen! You can have a beautiful, wonderful, memorable day, by all means! But the odds of it happening all in one day — ceremony and reception of your dreams done and dusted in one day within your fiance's first 90 days in the country — the odds of all of that happening at once aren't great. This is the recipe for stress. You're already stressed, and you're already uncertain. You don't even know for sure if your partner is going to be here in time, which is a story for another chapter. But the most important thing in this, this cake that you're making of your marriage is the two people who are getting married, right? So what I would about all that perfect day stuff that you want to do is to hold on to that, think of it as this perfect — actually, I kind of hate the word perfect — think of it as this wonderful reception that you're going to have and put it aside to say like, we're going to do that later.

So my suggestion is as soon as possible, as your partner enters the country, get married, do it legally. Go to a courthouse, have a friend or a relative, get one of those Internet ordination things (is that what it's called?) and marry you. That's what we did. My mom married us. It was beautiful. We loved it. And we had our parties later. We had one in the US, we had one in Turkey, and they were both a blast. But the amount of stress that was relieved just by separating that and getting married as soon as possible so that we could keep the immigration process going so that my husband could end up being able to work sooner than later — it was an incredible amount of stress that was relieved and I can't recommend it enough.

Separate the Ceremony from the Reception

I've kind of already given away how I feel about separating your ceremony and your reception. Spoiler alert: I love it! It is one of my favorite things that we did in our whole K-1-wedding-green-card process. **The short version of my advice is to get married one day and party all you want on a different day or days.**

With the time limit of the K-1 visa, it's really hard to get all of the guests that you want together before it's too late, especially if half of those guests are in another country. I'm guessing half of those guests *are* in another country because if you're applying for a K-1 visa, then your partner's not from the same country as you. Automatically, the logistics involved to get everyone together are complicated. That's why I would suggest having that big celebration later when you can get all of your loved ones together and even to consider having a party in each place if yo choose to do that.

The more time you can take to plan this wedding party, the more stress you'll ideally be able to relieve. You can do it months later, you can do it years later, or if you decide you don't want to have the party at all, then you can simply skip it. The important thing is just that you get legally married and you can figure the rest out at your leisure.

Why do this? What's the hurry?

One really important thing to be aware of with the K-1 visa (and you may already know this) is that the person who has a K-1 visa cannot work until they receive their employment authorization. That is something that happens only after you're married. Once you're married, you file paperwork for Adjustment of Status, to move from being a K-1 visa holder to a green card holder/permanent resident. Concurrently with that paperwork for Adjustment of Status, you can also file for Advanced Parole and Employment Authorization.

Those are two very important things because Advanced Parole means your partner can leave the US and Employment Authorization means he or she can work. In my experience, both of those things go a long way to helping someone feel like they have autonomy and they're not trapped in a situation where they're stranded someplace, unable to work and unable to leave — well, actually, they can leave, but if they do, then they can't come back without starting from the beginning of a new visa process. Try to imagine how that feels and then prioritize getting past that feeling together. This person that you love is going to need something to do, right? Whether it's important for both of you that they have an income or not, they probably want to have something to do with their time and it's going to be a lot easier for that to happen once they are authorized to work and travel. This right here is why I feel so, so, so very strongly about separating your ceremony and reception and that's why I'm probably never going to shut up about about it.

Don't Commit to a Date Yet

Another piece of important advice that you *may* find me repeating is not to commit to a wedding date yet. Until you and your partner are in the same country, don't pick a wedding date, put it on the calendar, print your invitations, and start mailing them to people. Okay?

This is something that could potentially cause you a whole lot of stress. Even if the visa has been granted, it's not enough until your partner is in the country with you. There are many things to consider and they all are significant. Passports can get lost or delayed in the mail, for example. When my husband and I were newly engaged in Turkey, we were planning a trip to the UK. His interview went well, he got his visa approved, and everything seemed great. We knew the visa was approved and on its way to us, so we went ahead and booked our flights. As our departure got closer, we were tracking his passport and visa on the shipping website and thought it was all fine and good until the carrier closed for an extended holiday. While his passport was in the city that we were living in, we were not able to get to it. So, learn from my mistake and don't do what I did. Have the passport in your hand before you book a flight and certainly before you set a wedding date in the immediate future.

This is just one factor to consider in the travel game. Of course air travel comes with the potential for delays or cancellations, and connecting through other countries only adds another layer to that. So please, please don't dismiss these realities. I certainly don't recommend inviting all of your friends to meet you at the arrivals gate at the airport for an impromptu wedding ceremony and basing the time on what's printed on your partner's ticket.

We've also got to think about the weather. Being born and raised in the Midwest (any Michiganders reading this?), I'm very familiar with snowy winters that prevent people from being able to go places. I've had too many missed Christmases with our extended family to not believe that weather is a significant factor worth considering any time you're making plans.

There is also the matter of potential problems at the port of entry. When the non-citizen partner enters the US, it is not guaranteed that the visa it will be accepted. That's something that USCIS is always careful to state — "this does not guarantee you entry." It still depends on the agent who accepts your passport, looks at your visa and then decides if you come in or not. I don't know how common this problem is but it is absolutely worth considering. As an aside, this is also why I like the idea of having the non-citizen partner's port of entry being the same airport where you'll be able to meet him or her. This wasn't possible for us — we ended up having to do some rerouting because flying through Canada was not an option for my husband without getting an additional visa. His port of entry ended up not being the same airport where I was and it caused me some extra stress because if something had gone wrong, I wasn't there. I was four hours away waiting for him at the next airport. If at all possible, it's nice to be there, just a quick phone call away if for some reason you need to be. But I digress! Back to weddings...

The Most Important Ingredients

What are the two most important ingredients for any wedding? The venue? A killer band? Why, of COURSE, they're the two people who are getting married! Right? To be clear, I didn't share all of those potential things that can go wrong just to be a naysayer making you feel like everything is going to fall apart, your life is doomed, and the world is a terrible place. Not at all. Rather, I did it to remind you that **all that really matters for the wedding is the two of you**. So focus on that. Put your energy into getting the two of you in the same place and wait to commit to any kinds of plans (or at least nonrefundable plans).

> *The two most important components of any wedding are the people getting married. If you aren't sure they'll both be there, then wait to commit to any plans. You can't get married over Skype.*

Protect Your Boundaries

In this stressful time, it's important to remember to protect your boundaries, even (or perhaps especially) with loved ones. Remember that your wedding, the ceremony, and the celebration is about you and your partner, the two of you. However, that doesn't mean that everyone else won't have an opinion because they absolutely will. You cannot avoid that and you cannot prevent that. But what you can do is work on establishing or protecting boundaries around your relationship so that those opinions don't end up becoming more important than your own opinions and wants and needs.

This is something really important — boundaries are going to serve you through the rest of your relationship. The two of you need to establish yourselves as your own entity, your own little family, and not just an extension of one of your families. You can start practicing this with the wedding. If someone tells you that you have to do something — you've got to wear a white dress, you got to toss the garter, or you've got to participate in any kind of tradition that makes you want to say, "Nope! That's not for me." — then this is a great opportunity to practice your boundaries. You can learn how to bless it and release it by saying, "Thank you. I appreciate your input. I'll consider it." Then you can consider it and make your own decision.

It's totally fine if you decide not to do something that someone else wants you to do it. You and your partner have two cultures, two lives, two sets of hopes and dreams and wishes and fears to blend already. It's not really necessary to add more into that mix — like any soon-to-be-married couple, you've got enough work cut out for you already!

Reality Check

As you're thinking about the money that you might want to spend on your wedding, it's a good idea to get a little reality check and remember (or become aware for the first time) that immigration is expensive. The numbers as of January 2020 are as follows, though of course I recommend checking with the State Department and USCIS for up-to-date information. Today, the filing fee for the I-129F is $535, and one that is approved the fee for the K-1 visa application is $265. After that, there will be additional expenses in country, and it will depend on where you are and what embassy you are doing your application through. For us, this included paying for a health check and immunizations, though it could potentially be more or less depending on your situation.

Once you're married, you'll file an application for Adjustment of Status for getting a conditional green card. At the time of this writing, the filing fee for that is $1,225. That includes the biometrics fee that needs to be paid in order to collect fingerprints and other data and is mandatory. All of these applications add up to quite a bit, so it is important to be aware of them, especially the AOS fee which will come after your wedding. Make sure if you've got a set budget for your wedding and your ceremony and your reception and your honeymoon, for example, to be aware that at the end of all that fun, you're going to need to have the money for that filing fee.

Exercises

Use this space to write down any breakthroughs about what **you** and your fiance(e) want for your wedding, letting go of the expectations of others. How can you protect your boundaries regarding your wedding plans?

5

Planning Your Ceremony

All right, let's get into the fun. This chapter is all about planning your ceremony, and we're diving right in.

What's Your Style?

It's important to start by thinking about your own style, so let's start by mulling over a few questions. When I ask, "What's your style?" it's important to remember that the "your" here is plural. We are talking about both you and your partner and these decisions are not just up to one of you. Now, you're going to need to think about your style and preferences for the ceremony and the reception, especially if you are deciding whether or not to keep them together or to separate them, so you can answer some of these questions on your own. These are just a few examples of questions to start with, and you can keep on going from there.

What will you wear to your wedding? Are you thinking more traditional, a white dress or a suit? Or are you thinking something that's unique to you and your style or your culture or your partner's culture?

Who will perform the ceremony? Will you have it done by a member of the clergy, a justice of the peace, or (spoiler alert: this one is my favorite and what we did) a family member or friend? My mom got ordained online so that she was able to perform our ceremony for us, which was really lovely and personal.

Which traditions do you love? This includes traditions from your culture, your partner's culture, or something that's new to you that you just would love to incorporate into your ceremony and your reception. Do you like the tradition where you cut the cake and then smash it on each other's faces or does that make you want to run for the hills? Do you like the garter toss or a bouquet toss or do you think that those are really uncool and you don't want to do them? Think about what's traditional in both of your cultures and make notes of the things that you would really love to incorporate on your day.

What dessert will you serve? This is a big deal, right? Some people have really strong opinions about what is or isn't an appropriate wedding cake. It doesn't necessarily have to be a three layer cake or whatever else you been told, but what is it that you both love and that will be memorable for you? Do you want to keep a portion of your dessert to freeze and eat on your one year anniversary? I can't say I've done it, but that seems to be a legitimate question, at least in the US.

What music will you play? Do you want to have traditional music play during the ceremony? What do you want to dance to at the reception? Maybe one of you is from a culture that has a really unique musical style that might seem unusual to the other side of the family. Regardless, if it's important to you, then play it. You get to choose what music you love, of course, just as you get to choose what you want to play to celebrate your new marriage.

What are your honeymoon plans? This is important. I'm sure you know that an international honeymoon will not be an option right after the wedding, right? As the non-citizen partner of your couple has not yet been granted Advanced Parole, it's not going to be possible for him or her to return to the US if you leave. Consider your options within the US or plan to postpone if you're determined to go somewhere international. Then think about what's important to you — do you want to do something small, like spending a weekend in a cottage, or do you definitely want to go spend multiple weeks on a tropical beach? Obviously this is totally up to you, but all of these are important things to consider and they also all play into your wedding budget as well.

You Can Keep it Secret/Low-Key...

Let's revisit a concept here for a minute. If you really love the idea of having everything happen on one special day and you can't let it go, that's totally okay. You can have a low-key ceremony now and you can have another one at your big party with everybody there. You aren't even obligated to tell anyone about your low-key ceremony if you are afraid that it won't make your public celebration as special as it deserves to be. **The thing is that you don't owe this to anyone.** So if Mom, Dad, Grandma, your great uncle, or anyone else can't handle the idea of you not having the big wedding they always dreamed of for you, that's about that person and not about you. If you think somebody is not going to want to come to your delayed celebration because you're already legally married, you can at least give them the option to come. You can certainly put it out there and see what they think and they might surprise you. You might find that people aren't as traditional as you think they are and you might find that they are too. Give them the option to say "yes" rather than speaking for them and assuming they aren't interested. Whatever the outcome, you'll be okay, especially if you continue to work on establishing healthy expectations and boundaries.

Now as far as the matter of anniversaries, let's address a teeny tiny elephant that may or may not be in the room. I'll admit that when I initially considered that we might have to separate our ceremony and our reception, I was really concerned about which anniversary to celebrate. I know that might sound very silly, but it was something that I was culturally conditioned to believe: you have one special anniversary and you celebrate it every year. And that is that. Heck, there are even specific gifts you're "supposed" to celebrate it with each year! I didn't really know how it would work if we separated things and had multiple significant dates in our marriage. The truth and reality is that **you get to choose what you celebrate**. You can celebrate the anniversary of every single thing that you could possibly want to celebrate...or not. You can celebrate your ceremony, your reception(s), or you can even pick a new, neutral date when none of those things happened and celebrate that! You can celebrate all of these dates, you can celebrate none of them, or you can do anything in between. There is no hard or fast rule about how many anniversaries you're allowed to celebrate.

Exercises

What's your style? What does your dream wedding day look like? What things are non-negotiable, and what are you willing to compromise about?

What do you think about separating your ceremony and reception? How does that thought make you feel?

6

Planning Your Reception

Let's continue on the same train of thought from the previous chapter and focus here on planning your reception.

We'll begin this chapter with my own personal myth busting. I'm not going to lie, weddings are surrounded by myths. They are deeply ingrained in our culture and history, and as a result there are many commonly held beliefs about what has to happen at a wedding. I'm referring here to traditions. *A bride must wear a white dress. The engagement ring or wedding rings or whatever kind of ring thing you have, it must be a massive diamond. The person who buys that ring must spend at least a month's salary on it. You have to do a garter toss. You have to do a bouquet toss, you have to do a dollar dance, you have to wear something blue or you'll have bad luck. Ahh, that's the secret. You have to do **anything** someone tells you just so you can avoid bad luck in your marriage.*

Well, here's the thing about all of that. There are traditions in your culture, there are traditions in your partner's culture, and there are traditions for weddings in probably every culture of the world. In your marriage, you are blending two cultures together. You have all of the traditions from one side of the family, as well as all of the traditions from the other side of the family. Is it really going to be possible and desirable for you to take each and every tradition from both of your cultures and incorporate them into your wedding? If that's something that you want to do and feel strongly about, then more power to you! But if it's something that you feel obligated to do because other people expect you to, then who are other people to tell you what to do with your wedding? You figure out what it is that's important to you and run with it. We've talked a bit about boundaries already, but the important thing is that you are happy with your celebration and it's meaningful to you. If what will make you happy is doing things that are important to your grandma or your great uncle, then by all means do those things. But ask yourself and your partner first and foremost: what's meaningful to us, and what's important to us? How can we celebrate in a way that's true to who we are?

As an example of this, for our wedding and celebration, one thing that really wasn't significant to me was the idea of wearing a white dress. When we got married in our tiny wedding ceremony I wore a green dress because it was Christmas Eve and it was beautiful and I loved it and I was happy and it was comfortable. At our reception in the US, I wore a white beach dress my husband had bought me the same day we got engaged. At our final celebration in Turkey, I did wear a massive white wedding gown with a hoop skirt and everything because it was important to my in-laws. That's an example where I tried to be true to my own style, but when it came to being with our family in Turkey, there were a number of other factors that came in to play. We had been away, I knew this was important to our Turkish family, and I knew it would make me happy to do what was important to them. I'm not interested in turning everything into a battle or expecting the world and everyone in it to conform to my expectations. And hey, I did still find ways to make it my own — I wore my favorite comfy shoes under my dress, but with a 6-foot radius hoop skirt no one else even had to know. If you can, stretch yourself a bit — what do you want to challenge, what do you want to accept, and what is worth fighting to have it your way? These answers will be different for everyone, something I find especially beautiful about a community like ours.

Can't Figure Out Where? Have Two!

If you can't figure out where to have your reception, why not consider having two celebrations, one in each of your home countries? If your friends and family are far apart, this is a great solution! Naturally, this is almost surely the truth if you're going through the K-1 visa process, unless you live on one side of the Canadian or Mexican border and they live on the other side, just a short drive away. It seems much more likely the distance between your families isn't drivable, so you might want to consider having two wedding receptions.

Otherwise, if you only have one celebration, how do you choose where to do it? How can you decide if it should be in your home country or your partner's home country? You have to consider who is able to travel or if you have family members on one or both sides of the family who may not have a passport or may not be comfortable with air travel. How expensive will it be to have half of your family travel to where you are? If that's not a financial barrier for you, then why are you even reading this paragraph? But if it's going to be easier and remove stress from you and from your family to have two celebrations, then I think it's worth considering. You can have one in each setting people can come to the geographically convenient one or even to both if they're able.

It takes a lot of pressure off when you don't say, "You've got to come to the other side of the world to celebrate my marriage or else you truly don't care about me." We can feel a lot of pressure as friends or as family members if we're not able to be there for our loved ones on their special day, but it can be prohibitively expensive if it is far away.

One note I would like to add with this is the importance of letting go of details, especially for a wedding that's happening with the in-law side of your family. There might be traditions that you don't totally understand that aren't totally meaningful to you, but if they are special and meaningful to that side of your family, then it's at least worth considering participating in those traditions.

Let me share an example of this to illustrate my point. I am somebody who is terrified of dancing in public. It is not something that I enjoy doing, it's not something that makes me feel comfortable, and it's not something that I've ever done happily. Now, because my husband's family is Turkish, I do dance Turkish style in public, which is stepping in a big circle with other people, while snapping your fingers. It's perfect for me. It's such a great, unexpected perk of marrying into a culture that has a defined idea of what dancing means, unlike American pop culture where dancing can mean anything in a wide range of styles.

Now, when we had our wedding, we incorporated the henna night into the wedding and there's a tradition there where the groom sits on a chair and the bride dances around him with a clay jar in her hands full of candy. She dances in a circle around his chair and then eventually smashes it on the ground. And I was having cold sweats about this. I was thinking, "Not only do I have to dance in front of all of these people, but I also have to smash something!" As somebody who had a very unsuccessful stint in martial arts in my teen years, I was also surprisingly afraid of smashing things in public. I had been to one demonstration as a *taekwondo* student where I had to break a board by kicking it, and it was a massive, massive failure. I think it took three tries and by the time it finally broke, I think the two men holding the board were the ones who broke it with their hands, not actually my foot. So for the henna night, I was concerned, "What if I can't smash it on the first try? How embarrassing is this going to be for me, for my husband, for everybody watching?"

Choosing to participate in that and to not let my fears dictate that I couldn't do it was one of the things that I carry with me to this day when I want to believe that I'm brave and can do hard things. While it all turned out fine in the end, I essentially had an out-of-body experience dancing in front of hundreds of people, anxiety kicked into high gear the whole time. But I knew how important it was to my in-laws, and I knew that it would mean something to my husband for me to do this. And on a personal level, I really didn't want to be that person who was gave in to my fears and insisted on having things done my way. As a result, it ended up being one of my favorite memories from our whole series of wedding celebrations.

*Disclaimer: This is not to say that all the best weddings require facing your fears. No need to incorporate heights, small enclosed spaces, or a clown officiant unless there's some greater meaning and motivation to do so.

Use Technology

In the midst of all the decisions and celebrations, it's important to remember to connect with loved ones who are unable to be present in person. One thing that's great for connecting both sides of your family is technology. The reality is that there are people who will miss your ceremony and/or your reception. It's just the truth, and it comes with the territory of K-1 visa life. So if you want to include people, you don't want them to feel left out, and you don't want them to feel like you've chosen one side of the family over the other, then let technology be your friend.

Incorporating technology to bring our worlds together for a celebration was something that we decided to do very spontaneously. As we were preparing for our wedding ceremony, everybody was feeling kind of subdued because it was only going to be with a very small group of people, just with my nuclear family. And as much as we loved that group of people, it really didn't feel great to not be sharing this experience with all the people that we cared about. We didn't really want to livestream our wedding all over our social media for the whole world to see; we still wanted to intentionally invite people to it. So the day (or possibly even hours) before our wedding, we created a private Facebook group and we invited everyone who couldn't be there to join the group. Then, we livestreamed our ceremony in that private group. We had ten people (including four children) together for the ceremony, so one of those people had the job of holding the phone and keeping the livestream going. It ended up being something that was really special for the people who "attended" that day, as we learned from their comments and champagne selfies that day and in the years since as they recall it with us. It helped bridge that gap of disconnection and made us feel like we were all sharing in this special experience. We treasure that memory, as well as the video that we can watch again, seeing our loved ones' comments pop up in real time.

Exercise

How can you maximize the number of loved ones that you celebrate with? Will you have two receptions? Use technology to include the other side of the family? Write down your ideas here.

7

It's Up to You

As we close out our time together, I'm slipping in a few more ideas that didn't quite fit anywhere else. And I'd like to start this chapter and end this book by reminding you not to take anything I say so seriously that it causes you stress. All the ideas you read here (like all the unwanted input you may have received from people in your life) are just ideas, and the ultimate authorities in your relationship and in your wedding are you and your partner alone.

Maybe you can do it all in one day...

The reality is, even though I say that separating the ceremony and the reception is the only way to go for me, it doesn't mean it has to be for you. Maybe you *can* actually do it all in one day. If it's a priority to you, there's no reason to say that you cannot.

Should you choose to plan one big ceremony and celebration, there are some things you'll need to consider given the short time frame you're working with. To start with, you can alert your potential guests to how quickly this will all unfold. While you might not be able to tell them to save a specific date, you can keep them updated on your K-1 progress and remind them that your wedding date will be within 90 days of you and your partner being reunited in the US.

For the venue you might have to get nontraditional if your favorite traditional options aren't available at short notice. If that's the case, then think outside the box and see what other options there are. If it's a nice time of year, maybe you could have an outdoor ceremony. If it's colder out then maybe you want to explore hotels or a conference center or whatever local options are available. In my hometown, there's an out-of-service train depot that's great for events, so get creative and see what you can work with. Heck, we ended up having a reception at the bike shop! Think of what places exist, as well as the connections that you already have.

As far as catering, you can ask around for availability. You can see who's got the time and who might be willing to work with you and look for refundable deposits as well. For decorations, get creative. What can you learn how to do on Pinterest? What can you prepare in advance? Maybe instead of fresh flowers you can use something that will last or something that you can make ahead of time. The more things that you can take out of out of the equation for dealing with the day of, the better off you'll be.

Maybe instead of ordering paper invitations, you can use online ones instead. There's nothing tacky about that when you're planning a wedding in such a short span of time. You could print or handletter your own invitations, too. You might have to get creative, and time and money can both be limiting factors, so try to be as realistic as possible.

You can also be prepared to pay somebody. Your options are either to get creative with most of this stuff or be prepared to pay someone. If your budget is limited, then the more that you can do and the more that you can utilize your family members and your friends, the better off you'll be. If your budget is more flexible, then by all means you can find people to pay to do all of these things. For music, if you don't have access to a DJ or to a band or something that might be your first choice, then make a playlist of songs that you love — your favorite songs, songs that you enjoy dancing to, and songs that are meaningful to you. You can designate someone to be in charge of it, if you'd like to take that responsibility off your plate.

It's also worth noting that when you're contacting service providers in these different areas, you can tell them your story. Maybe they don't want to hear the whole story but you can at least explain that you are going through the K-1 visa process and explain what that is. Many people are familiar with it now, especially with pop culture and the "90 Day Fiance" TV shows and that might open doors for you a bit. They might be willing to be more flexible for you, considering the nature of your situation.

The bottom line

The bottom line for planning all of these special memories and getting it all done within that 90 day window is to keep it small(ish). You don't have to get married with only 10 people there including yourself and your partner — though, fun fact: that's what my husband and I did. You can of course include more people in your special day. To help with this, get your loved ones involved. There's no need to do everything yourself. I will say my dad took on the role of wedding planner for our reception in a way that I never thought he was capable of, and it was such a gift. It was such a blessing, especially considering all of the other pressures and stressors that were going on at that time. And of course, the most important thing is to remember what the day, whether it's one day or multiple days, remember what it is really about. **Remember the point of this day is celebrating love and beginning a new stage of your relationship together.**

Sure you can

I've spent a lot of time telling you what you should and shouldn't do and what works and doesn't work. If any of this has you feeling like, "Ahh, I really wanted to do [fill-in-the-blank], but KC told me I can't so now I can't," I'm just going to remind you that really truly, *you* are the captain of your own ship. So here's what I want to say: SURE. You can! Sure you can.

I might say you can't pick a wedding date on faith that your partner's going to be there in time. But, sure, you can! Sure you can. There are a few things I would advise you to consider (and I'm going to list them out here because I can't help it), but who am I to say that your faith isn't as important as my advice? That doesn't sound like me.

So if you're thinking of doing just that, picking a date on faith and sticking to it, here are a few things I'd advise you to keep in mind. First off, refundable deposits are important. You might feel like you just know this is going to work and you don't need to play it safe — I just don't want to see you lose a big chunk of change. So if you need to put down a deposit for something, talk to the person who you're arranging that with and explain the situation. Maybe you can say see if for some reason you aren't able to hold the event on the day that you're booking, they'll be willing to let you apply that deposit to a different date to be decided upon later.

Other things to think about include transit. Other people who might want to come to your wedding, are they going to be able to get visas if they're from another country or are they going to be able to get flights? And because I'm from Michigan, I say one really important thing to consider where your guests are concerned is the weather. We got married on Christmas Eve and one factor that kept us from trying to make it a big party and inviting everyone was definitely the weather. I know I can't count on people being able to travel to me in Michigan in December;

sometimes the roads are terrible and it can significantly change your plans. I don't want somebody that I love to get stuck in a bad situation because there's too much snow on the road. This may be a moot point if you're getting married in summer, but it's a good mental exercise to at least consider the factors that are out of your control. I'm not advising you to make a laundry list of all the things that could possibly go wrong, but thinking through a few things (and coming up with contingency plans) can help keep your stress in check.

Finally, it's always a good idea not to take your partner's visa and travel plans for granted until the visa is in hand and he or she is on the plane. This can be a cause for concern if your partner is from what USCIS considers a "high fraud" country, but for anyone anywhere, it's always possible to have issues getting those essential documents into your hands. I've had my share of visa drama, and I've learned the hard way that even having a tracking number for your visa might not be strong enough to justify booking a short notice flight.

Final thoughts

I appreciate you sharing your time with me, and I hope this guide has been helpful to you on your journey. My wish for you and your partner is to be reunited, happy, free of stress, and on the path to creating a special day or days that's true to you and your love. Don't be a stranger — come share your journey with us over at BorderlessStories.com.

Exercise

Use this free space to write down any more notes or thoughts, whether that's about prioritizing budget over a massive party (or vice versa), ways to utilize the talents of your loved ones on your big day, or an idea for a fun date night in the midst of all the stress.

About the Author

KC McCormick Çiftçi is the founder of Borderless Stories, where she provides coaching for people in intercultural relationships, leads a membership community, and hosts a podcast about loving across borders. Borderless Stories was created when KC and her Turkish husband were beginning the K-1 fiance visa process while navigating an intercultural, international relationship. Connect with her at www.BorderlessStories.com to keep in touch.

Also by KC McCormick Çiftçi

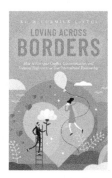

Loving Across Borders

https://www.borderlessstories.com/loving-across-borders

"Loving Across Borders" is a user's guide for an intercultural relationship. Falling in love with someone from another country is a beautiful thing, but it comes with a unique set of obstacles, from cultural differences to immigration and plenty in between. In this book, learn the skills to navigate these challenges and create a dream relationship.

Made in United States
Orlando, FL
27 June 2022

19218217R00036